Presented to

_____

by

_____

Date

_____

EVERYDAY
PRAYERS
for
Women

DIMENSIONS
FOR LIVING

NASHVILLE

EVERYDAY PRAYERS FOR WOMEN

Copyright © 1993 by Dimensions for Living

99 00 01 02 — 10

This book is printed on recycled, acid-free paper.

ISBN 0-687-07534-3

The Steps of Prayer is adapted from HOW TO PRAY,
E. Stanley Jones. Copyright © 1943 by Whitmore & Stone.

Prayers on pages 49–63 are adapted from BLESSINGS
FOR CHURCH OCCASIONS, Ruth C. Ikerman. Copyright © 1987 by Abingdon Press. Used by permission.

MANUFACTURED IN THE UNITED STATES OF AMERICA

Contents

The Steps of Prayer

First, decide what you really want. The "you" is important. It must not be a vagrant part of you wandering into the prayer hour with no intention of committing yourself to your prayer request. You cannot pray with a part of yourself and expect God to answer, for God hears what the whole of you is saying . . .

Second, decide whether the thing you want is a Christian thing. God has shown us in Christ what the divine character is like. God is Christ-like. He can only act in a Christ-like way. He cannot answer a prayer that would not fit in with his character . . .

Third, write it down. The writing of the prayer will probably help you in self-committal. For, if you write it, you will probably mean it. The writing of it will also save you from hazy indefiniteness . . . There will come a time, of course, when you may not need to write things down, for they will have written themselves in you . . .

Fourth, still the mind. The stilling of the mind is a step in receptivity. Prayer is pure receptivity in the first stage. "As many as received him, to them gave he power." If you come to God all tense, you can get little . . .

Now you are ready for the fifth step: Talk with God about it. "Talk with God," not "Talk to God," for it is a two-way conversation. And the most vital part may be, not what you will say to God, but what God will say to you . . .

There is a sixth step: . . . At this point be silent to hear God again, and see if he makes any suggestions to you about your part in answering the prayer. If definite suggestions come to you, then promise that you will carry them out . . .

Seventh, do everything loving that comes to your mind about it! This step is important, for it is a cleansing and clarifying step. The word *loving* is important. The first fruit of the Spirit is "love," and if the suggestion does not fit in with love, then don't do it.

Wait for the suggestion that does fit in.

Eighth: thank God for answering in his own way. God will answer that prayer. No prayers are unanswered. But God may answer "no" as well as "yes." "No" is an answer, and it may really be next in order leading on to a higher "yes."

There is a ninth step: Release the whole prayer from your conscious thinking. Don't keep the prayer at the center of your conscious thinking. It may become an anxiety-center. Let it drop down into the sub-conscious mind and let it work at that greater depth. Then there will be an undertone of prayer in all you do, but there will be no tense anxiety. Dismissing it from the conscious mind is an act of faith that, having committed it to God you leave it in his hands, believing he will do the best thing possible . . .

E. Stanley Jones

On My Mother's Birthday

Today is my mother's birthday, Lord. Now that I'm a mother myself I realize how important this day was not only for my mother, but for her mother as well. Even on our most special days—our birthdays—we are all so connected.

Thank you for my mother, O God, and for her long life. Grant her many more years with us and with the grandchildren she loves so much. Give her health and strength of body and mind. Hold her in your hands.

Show me how to love her as she has loved me—always and without reservation, for all our days. AMEN.

A Child's First Day at School

Dear God, here is _____, ready for her first day at school. She has been counting the days. She is so thrilled.

Be with her today when she goes into unfamiliar rooms, when she sees new faces (make them kind faces!), when she stands in the lunch line, when she is on the playground. Keep her close to you as she learns and grows and makes friends. Protect her from harm. Watch over her on the way to and from school. And as she becomes part of a larger world, help me to let her go and gain experience that she will need to become a responsible part of your creation. AMEN.

For a New Mother

My friend's baby has been born! Her first one. How thrilled and touched she sounds! She has finally witnessed a miracle.

Thank you, Lord, for my friend and for this beautiful new life you have entrusted to her and her husband. Today she praises you and thanks you for her precious gift. Bless this new family with your grace that they might grow ever close to you and to one another. Be with my friend in her joy and in her fatigue; in her nights of fitful sleep; when the baby is crying and she doesn't know why. Help her recall the awe and wonder of this day and to rejoice at the privilege of being an instrument of your ongoing creation. AMEN.

For a Busy Day with Children

Father, thank you that I am also a parent. I'm looking forward to this busy day that will be filled with the chatter and laughter of my children. May I catch their enthusiasm and may their interests infect my own spirit so that I, too, may have a childlike eagerness for the events of the day. Give us patience if the day grows long and tempers wear thin. May we end the day with eagerness to spend another together. AMEN.

When Children Quarrel

O gracious God, Father of us all, I ask you for help and guidance when my children quarrel. Often I wonder how these children, loved as they are, can be so unloving and unlovely. Their teasing, provoking, and fighting hurt me, Lord, and make me lose my temper as well. Grant me patience and understanding. Help me to establish within our home and family an atmosphere of harmony, but help me too to remember that my children are not adults and that trying their strength is part of growing up. Keep me sane, Lord, calm, and unruffled, ready to quiet, to comfort, and to smile. AMEN.

When Caring for an Ill Relative

It's going on five months now, Lord, and I have been taking care of _____ every day. Sometimes I am so tired, but I know she would do the same for me.

So many things to deal with, Lord. Not only the physical challenges and stress she and I both face—she in her illness and I in this new responsibility of caretaker—but a slowly evolving understanding I have not breathed to anyone: that she will not recover. I cannot quite accept this yet, and I pray every day that you might help her recover. "Not my will. . . ."

Help us, Lord. Help us accept the challenges we face and to draw strength from you. Help us remember how you suffered for us. Help us remember how you cried for your friend Lazarus. And when the time comes for us to face you, remember us. AMEN.

For a Childless Friend

Lord, you have given my friend a very special cross to bear. She is unable to have children. I remember how excited she was that night when she called to tell me she was pregnant. But she lost the baby a few weeks later, than another, then another.

It's been three years now. She's forty years old. I have had two beautiful daughters in the meantime. I thank you that our friendship has lasted through these experiences.

But for my friend, Lord, she's the one who really wanted children all those years when I was unsure. She prayed and prayed. But you have other plans for her. I hope someday before too long you might help her understand. Some days she is so preoccupied she thinks she is losing her mind.

Please be with her, O God. You have given a great gift to her in her husband. He loves her; he listens to her; he supports her; he grieves with her for their children who might have been.

Help me to be the best friend I can be. AMEN.

For a Co-worker Who Lost Her Job

Dear Lord, what a difficult day this has been! My co-worker was terminated. She called me right away. I can hardly remember what I said to her, but you helped me; I do know that. I thank you for that.

About my friend, Lord. Her family needs her income. She has many talents. But her self-esteem has suffered a terrible blow. She will need confidence in the days ahead, and she will need strength and patience, and she will need you.

Be with her when she finds it difficult to pray. Give her courage and strength when she starts the unenviable task of job-hunting. Help her remember that she is precious to you, invaluable to you. She needs you now, more than she might know. In your mercy, sustain her. AMEN.

To Be a Comforter

What do *you* do, Lord, when someone needs comfort. Send me? I want to, Lord. But I don't know how, and I am afraid.

You know just the right words to match the needs. You know just the right time to lend a touch. You know just the right facial expression to show love and concern.

But I know none of these. My words all seem so insignificant. My touches and my glances all seem so pointless. Do you still want me to go, to be a comforter?

Then, I need your guidance, Lord. Let your words be on my lips. Let your touch be upon my hand. Let the kindness and comfort of your face be upon mine.

And touch the heart of my loved one with understanding of my meaning. AMEN.

Prayer of an Expectant Mother

Dear heavenly Father, words cannot express the joy I feel in knowing that soon I will have a child. You have blessed my life in so many ways, but I am especially thankful for this special blessing. I am so anxious about the exciting changes taking place within me—physically, emotionally, mentally, and even spiritually. More than ever, Father, I feel your love filling me and enfolding me. Help me to entrust my worries to your care, particularly those worries about the health and safety of my baby. Thank you for the precious moments to be shared with my husband, family, and friends as we prepare for the birth of this child. I pray that as the child grows within me, I may grow in grace and love.

These things I ask in the name of your son, Jesus Christ. AMEN.

For a Friend Facing Divorce

Dear God, my friend just told me she's getting a divorce. How I hurt for her. She's lost in a whirlwind of emotions—anger, confusion, sorrow, depression, fear, and loneliness. I so want to comfort her and reassure her that everything will be all right, but the words are hard to find. Help me to be the kind of friend she needs right now—someone to be there for her and to listen. A sympathetic ear and outstretched arms are the best gifts I can give her. Surround her with understanding friends and family, Lord, and enfold her in the healing presence of your love. Fill her emptiness, and remind her that she is never alone. AMEN.

For My Husband

Dear Lord, I am so blessed to be married to the man I call my husband. "Husband" just doesn't seem to convey all that he is to me. He is my lover, my best friend, my confidant, my companion. There's no one else I'd rather laugh or cry with—in good times or bad. How grateful I am that you have brought us together. Yet I am only human, Lord. Sometimes I get angry or upset at something he has said or done—or *hasn't* said or done—and I lose my patience and my temper. Sometimes I concentrate on the qualities or habits I wish I could change rather than on his best qualities and endearing habits. Lord, at those times, help me to remember why I love him so much and to let go of the rest. AMEN.

On Interstate Driving

Dear God, I ask your special blessing today as I prepare myself for the drive to my workplace. Open my mind to the sights and sounds of busy people going about their daily routine. As I merge into the highway with the truck drivers, doctors, nurses, construction workers, school teachers, and business people help me to realize we all fit into your plan and have special duties for the day. May we all arrive safely to our varied destinations and the work that lies before us. I ask that you will be with each of us and return us safely to our homes and loved ones when our day is ended. AMEN.

For Caregiving to Parents

I ask your blessings, dear Lord, for new direction. You have always been with me even when I am unaware. Now, as new responsibilities face me in the role of care-giver for my aging parents, I know you are still with me. My parents taught me to always look to you for direction and guid-ance. Today as my parents look to me for their well-being, help me show the same love and tender care they have given me throughout my life. I realize the responsi-bilities are great, but the opportunity is there to become closer to them than ever before. May we grow more dear to each other and to you as we enter our new life together. This is my prayer. AMEN.

Receiving New Church Members

Dear Lord, today we received into our church family a new member eager to learn of your love and mercy. Help each of us show this person Christian love and fellowship that we may live and grow together in our spiritual lives. May this new member enrich our church by bringing new talents and interests into our lives. Give all of us grace to do work to glorify you, our God. AMEN.

Upon Taking Office

I thank you, Lord, for my friends and the fellowship we have. For bringing us together. For the love and compassion we have for each other. And for the confidence they have placed in me by electing me to this office.

Help me as I accept this office. Give me knowledge that I may use to guide us in our endeavors. Guide my thoughts that our meetings will have purpose and meaning. May the work we strive to do bring us together in love and goodwill. Grant us peace and harmony that the decisions we make together will be acceptable to each other and to you. In Jesus' name we pray. AMEN.

The Death of a Loved One

Dear tender shepherd, the one I loved is gone, the funeral over, friends and relatives departed. Now it is my task to write and to visit insurers, employers, and government officials; to give away or put away possessions; to begin anew. Be with me when so many things remind me of recent sorrow and earlier joys. As you once wept with your friends, so may I not be ashamed of my feelings during this time of remembering, when a picture, a letter or a card may bring alive another time. Thank you for the special memories of warmth and joy and for the promise that you will always be by my side. AMEN.

Before a Day's Work

Dear God, it's morning and I am preparing for another day at work. But before I go, I'd like to say thanks for waking me. Without your blessing of hearing, I would never have heard the alarm clock, birds outside my window, or even the traffic flow. Look after me as I go and see me safely to my place of work. AMEN.

For My Pastor's Family

Almighty God, families are a special blessing. Today I thank you for our pastor's family. They enrich so many lives in so many ways. Too often I forget to tell them how important they are to me and how much I appreciate their gifts of time, sacrifice, and service. Help me to find the right times and the right ways to show my appreciation and love for them. And help me to remember to tell others of this appreciation, so that they may be reminded to share their love as well. The expectations and demands on the pastor's family are great, and I pray that you will strengthen and sustain them through the difficult times. Pour out your blessings upon their home, and enable them to find time to nurture their family relationships and simply enjoy being together. In Jesus' name I pray. AMEN.

For Adventure in Everyday Living

O God, sometimes my days seem so dull and dreary. I fall into a rut, and I don't know how to climb out. Then, when I think I've found a way out, a way to infuse my life with excitement and renewed energy, I allow my fear of change to over-come me. Help me to break out of the end-less cycle of routine and predictability. Give me the courage and the faith to make each day an adventure, trusting in your steadfast love and protection. As I seek your guidance through prayer and medita-tion upon your word, I ask for the wisdom to make constructive changes in my life and to find new meaning and pleasure in the familiar. Knowing that you walk with me, I can face each new day with joyful anticipation. Thank you for your precious gift of life. AMEN.

A Vacation Prayer

Dear Lord, how I've waited for this vacation, and now it's finally here. Thank you, Lord, for the opportunity to take a break from my daily routine and to replenish my mind, body, and soul so that I may better serve you. Sometimes my expectations for vacations are unrealistic, and I find myself disappointed when things don't go my way. Help me not to worry about having the "perfect" vacation but to relax and enjoy every moment, whatever it may bring. I am grateful for the joys that await me—whether they be the beauty of your creation, recreation with family or friends, or peace and solitude. Watch over me and protect me as I travel, and bring me safely home again—refreshed and renewed. Amen.

Change in Life-style

Dear Lord, I see friends and acquaintances having to make changes in their life through no fault of their own: The husband who suddenly lost his wife of more than forty years. The wife who lost her husband to cancer after a long-suffering illness. The young wife and mother who lost her husband when he was shot by an irate tenant. The young boy who was disfigured for life by burns he sustained in a fire. The elderly who have lost their health and must be placed in a nursing home away from family and friends. I pray that your loving spirit will be with each of them as they enter into a life different from what they have known. Give them your grace and love. Comfort and sustain them when they feel all hope is lost. Lead and guide them when they feel so alone. Make me mindful of their special needs and give me the grace to show care and understanding. As our lives intertwine, show me how to give light to hopeless darkness, peace where there is turmoil, joy where there is sadness, and sympathy where there is sorrow. I ask this in the name of Jesus Christ, your son. AMEN.

Getting a New Preacher

Dear Lord, I pray that you will be with us as we receive into our church family your servant. Help us to show love and understanding when things are not always as they have been. May we be willing to receive instruction with an open mind and offer encouragement and compassion in hours of trial. May our membership increase and our Spirits be rekindled with the flame of the Holy Spirit. We pray that our new church family will find peace and joy in their new surroundings and cultivate memories of caring and loving friends. Make us aware of our needs for each other. Show us ways of removing stumbling blocks that will make your path easy to follow. Continue to be with us and bind us together in Christian love and service. For we ask it in the name of Jesus Christ, our Lord and Savior. AMEN.

For a Fruitful Prayer Life

Father, I come asking for help in my prayer life. Too often in the past my prayers have been only a form to be finished quickly so that I might get on to what I found more interesting. But I want my prayers to be more important than anything else. I want to make them so real and so vital that I can truly reach you and find strength and help for all areas of my life. Fill me with your Spirit and make me sincere and true in every way. AMEN.

To Be Thankful

Each day I see before me, Lord God, good reason for thanksgiving. Thank you for helping me find the happiness of quiet, simple things; for the contentment that comes from looking at a pot of flowers on a window ledge, at the light of an open fire on the hearth, or at color splashed across the evening sky. I pray for happiness and harmony within my home and with everyone I meet today. I pray for the happiness of being as nearly as I can at all times honest and sincere. I pray for the inner joy that Jesus knew. In his name. AMEN.

An Office Prayer

O Lord, thank you for this day, thank you for my job. Thank you for the many wonderful people you have placed me in the midst of at my workplace. Continue to direct me, and give me the strength and energy to be more productive. Encourage me to be an asset and not a liability. This is my prayer. AMEN.

For Disappointment

Lord, I've had such a disappointment today. Something I had hoped for, dreamed of, and yes, even prayed for is just not to be. I'm hurt and I'm angry. Help me to turn loose of this bitterness. Now I see only darkness and despair. Light your lamp within me, O Lord of Light. May I see clearly through this shadow that has fallen across my life. Remind me that just as the darkness of night only hides the day for a few hours, your light shines on behind the darkness of my difficulties and disappointments. AMEN.

A Daily Prayer

O God, let this be my prayer every day. Keep me from thinking any critical thought. Keep me from blaming others for anything. Keep me from being resentful. Keep me from saying or thinking any hurtful thing about anyone. Help me today and every day to think good and do good regardless of what anyone else may say or do. Spirit of all power and goodness, quiet my mind. Help me to be still enough to hear your voice. Help me to stop worrying and fretting. Help me to stop rebelling against circumstances. Help me to be like Jesus. AMEN.

To Be Worthy

Dear Lord, I turn away from you even when I know better. Forgive me again and again. Help me in the same way to forgive those who are disloyal to me. Build into my character a steadfast, unfailing spirit of goodwill toward everyone that cannot be influenced by anything that may be done to me. Make me your worthy child. AMEN.

For Carrying on Christ's Work

O Christ of the loving heart, who felt tenderness and compassion for all people, inspire me to feel the same, I pray. I do not have your power to heal and restore, but your Spirit lives within me. Smile through my face, speak through my voice, use me to help the sick and suffering, the discouraged and lonely. I want to carry on your work. AMEN.

For Giving God First Place

Dear God, when I am troubled or in trouble I come to you pleading for your help, but too often when things are going well I forget about you. Help me to see your loving guidance all the time—every hour, every day. Help me to stay close to you in prosperity and success just as in difficulty and failure. Help me to put you first in my life and to hold to that standard always. AMEN.

For God's Help in Relationships

All wise and loving God, you know how blind I can be to my own faults and how quick I sometimes am to see the faults of others. Clear my eyes, I pray, so that I can see both myself and others as we truly are. Help me to practice your great commandments to love you with all my being and to love others as myself. I can't do it alone, but with your help I can. Thank you for your unfailing love. AMEN.

A Budget-making Prayer

Dear Lord, I've just taken a long look through my checkbook and my calendar. It's sobering to realize where my time and my money are being spent. I know I need to plan for the use of my resources, and I need your help. It's difficult to balance desires, responsibilities, willingness to share, and personal discipline. Help me to be wise in the use of my present funds. Don't let me forget my obligations to church, community, my neighbor in the community, and my neighbor half a world away. Time, too, is a precious commodity. Help me plan for its wise use as well. Give me the perception to see where there is a special need. Help me to place emphasis not on the purchase of things but on investment in fruitful human service. AMEN.

A Christmas Shopping Prayer

O Christ Jesus whose birth so long ago began the traditions of today, thank you for the privilege of Christmas shopping. Help me to make even what could be a stress-filled time a time of wonder and excitement. Let me look at the Christmas decorations on city streets with the eyes of a child, to hear beyond the tinny sounds of recorded music the words of the story of your great gift to us. Make me patient in crowds, quick to smile and in some way bring a lift to the spirits of those whose work is heavier at this time. May each gift be chosen in your name and may I always give with love. AMEN.

With God

Begin the day with God:
Kneel down and say a prayer;
Lift up your heart to God's abode
And seek God's love to share.

Go through the day with God,
Whate'er your work may be;
Where'er you are—at home, abroad,
God still is near to thee.

Conclude the day with God:
Your sins to God confess;
Trust in the Lord's atoning blood,
And plead God's righteousness.

Lie down at night with God,
Who gives to all sweet sleep,
And when you treat the vale of death
God will you guard and keep.

Author Unknown (adapted)

The Meaning of Prayer

A breath of prayer in the morning
Means a day of blessing sure—
A breath of prayer in the evening
Means a night of rest secure.

A breath of prayer in our weakness
Means the clasp of a mighty hand—
A breath of prayer when we're lonely
Means someone to understand.

A breath of prayer in rejoicing
Gives joy and added delight.
For they that remember God's goodness
Go singing far into the night.

There's never a year nor a season
That prayer may not bless every hour
And never a soul need be helpless
When linked with God's great power.

Author Unknown

Blessing for an Annual Church Dinner

Our dear loving heavenly Father, we are grateful for this opportunity of Christian fellowship with one another and with you. Please be very near this night to our dear shut-ins who are not able to meet with us physically, but whose hearts join with ours in hope and love for this church. We remember with warm hearts also the women and men who have shared our spiritual dreams and who are now gone from this earthly life.

We ask you to give us an abiding sense of your own continuous presence in times of change. May we each take from the past the blessing of joyous memories, and grant that the inspiration of this gathering may give us fresh energy for future activities in your kingdom.

Bless this food to our bodies and this fellowship to our hearts that we may serve you better in our homes, through this church, and in our community and nation. These mercies we ask in the precious name of your son, Jesus, our Lord and our Savior. AMEN.

Blessing for a Stewardship Meeting

Dear God, we would be willing stewards
of your bounty, ever grateful for the abun-
dance of goodness with which you fill our
hearts. We are aware of the great gifts of
health and energy to work day by day and
for the natural blessings of earth, air, and
water. Forgive us for the times we have
taken these elements for granted, forget-
ting that you are the giver of every good
and perfect gift.

Now as we come together to consider
our stewardship of such gifts, place in our
hearts generous motives of unselfish giving
as reflections of your wondrous gifts to us.
Grant us wisdom to know how best to
share our financial blessings with other
persons that they may be encouraged to
live Christian lives and, in turn, may be

enabled to bless others and to serve you better.

From this discussion, may we all come away with renewed appreciation of our daily blessings and fresh strength to find Christian solutions to today's problems. AMEN.

Blessing for a Foreign Missions Meeting

Dear God, we are mindful of the Bible's admonition to go and teach all nations and of the precious promise of your presence with all who go in your name to serve in foreign fields. Keep us ever aware of our ability to make our influence felt as Christians through the support we give to such mission projects. May we never forget the need for daily prayer to encourage and sustain those who serve in mission fields. May this interest be backed by our financial resources to the best of our budget's ability.

Give us guidance as we plan our giving in the light of the many needs of the world. May our hearts be so enlarged as to include others in our prayers and activities. Keep us from limited vision and expand our horizons to include Christian brothers and sisters in far corners of the world. Together may we all give you praise for your wondrous blessings of peace in the heart and ultimately, in the world. AMEN.

Blessing for a Choir Supper

Kind Lord, precious Lord, be very near to us as we gather in happy fellowship with choir members of our own church. Let harmony reign in all our hearts as together we partake of these blessings of food and conversation.

We thank you for the opportunities we have to carol your praises in weekly services, leading others to know the beauty and power of the precious heritage of church music. Let us always be aware of music as a ministry for present needs. May our music be extended into the lives of those who listen, that they may be encouraged when discouraged, strengthened when weak, and always enabled to face life anew with a song in their hearts.

Keep our voices and our lives in harmony with your will. AMEN.

Blessing for Monthly Group Meetings

Dear Father, as the time for our monthly meeting arrives, we are aware of how quickly the days and weeks speed past. We are grateful that we can meet today with our common interest in mind. Help us to make wise use of the time allotted for consideration of our business that your kingdom may be advanced by our activities in this area. Undergird our deliberations with a spirit of unity and with a deep desire to serve you better every day. Grant each heart here a blessing to carry home to enrich the days of work and play until we meet again. May each month find us further along on our journey of faith. In Jesus' name. AMEN.

Prayer for a Bible Study Class

Dear God, we thank you for this opportunity to learn about the Bible with the help of our fine teacher. Show us how to make the most of the time we spend together so that we may gain information and inspiration to live our lives better. We are grateful to be able to spend time with friends in this class and to have a chance to make new ones. Bless this class and our church. We ask this in Jesus' name. AMEN.

Prayer for an Outdoor Worship Service

God of the open air, we come to you grateful for the outdoors and all that it offers in the way of recreation and pleasure for all ages. We thank you also for our church, with its regular routine, and the members with whom we may share this informal outdoor fellowship.

Help us all to relax and know that we are indeed your children, welcome in all your world to enjoy the beauty of mountains, seashore, desert, trees, and flowers. In this relaxed setting, may our minds be free from trivia and clutter, so that we may see clearly our opportunities to serve you better. Grant us fresh energy and renewed zest to serve you better. Bless each of us and our church so that we may reach others for you. AMEN.

Blessing for Graduation Recognition

Dear Father, we come to this milestone in the lives of students with deep gratitude for the teachings of eternal truths in the Bible. We are grateful for this opportunity of fellowship that celebrates the achievements of the mind in learning about your wonderful world. We remember with appreciation all the parents who were the first teachers of these students, even before they met their first school teachers. And we would not forget the dedicated Sunday school teachers who in their limited weekly times have taught the rules of Christian behavior. Grant that from this happy occasion we may all draw fresh strength for further study in our homes and churches. AMEN.

Prayer for a Church Retreat

Father of us all, be very near to this group as our church family gathers for a retreat to renew our spiritual strength and to plan ahead for future growth. We would not walk before you, but ask you to lead us in all our discussions and in facing up to the problems and demands of the present age.

We are grateful for this opportunity to meet together away from the daily responsibilities of routine. Grant that from this fellowship may come new friendships and a heightened sense of our togetherness as Christians united in a common cause.

Let there be moments of lighthearted play and pleasure to balance our serious discussions and our planning for future events. May this be a time of strengthened spiritual resolve to live daily lives that testify to your power and saving grace. AMEN.

Prayer for a Church Anniversary

O gracious Lord, we give you thanks for the great blessing of your loving presence with our church across the changing years of Christian service. We are grateful for those founding members who cared enough about the verities of eternity to found this church in a first building of worship. We remember the later sacrifices of time and talent so that more adequate facilities could be provided for their children and grandchildren to learn about God and how to live as Christians. Today we ask anew for a special portion of your power that we may never become indifferent to the values of Christian fellowship, with one another and with the other churches in our beloved community. Even as we celebrate our commitment, help us to realize with humility our human frailties and to remember your promise that a thousand years with you are as but a day. Let our day be strengthened with the righteousness that comes from you. These mercies we ask in the name of your Son, Jesus, our Lord and our Savior. AMEN.

A Prayer for the New Year

Dear God, our minds and hearts turn in two directions as we recall the many blessings of the past year and look ahead to anticipated blessings of the year just beginning. None of us can know what joy or sorrow will come into our lives, but we are grateful for the reassurance that you will be with us whatever situations we face.

Hear our thanks for the lasting joys of precious memories that keep the past a part of the present. Help us so to live day by day that we may build new memories to bless the future with happiness.

May this be a year in which our hearts are enlarged to embrace those who need assurance of your love, and may we move forward serenely through days of fellowship with one another and with you. AMEN.

A Benediction

Dear God, our hearts are filled with thanks for the joy and blessing of fellowship with great minds and spirits through personal contacts, letters, books, music, travel, and all the many opportunities afforded by our church. Forgive us the times we have failed to take advantage of what is available to us in our weekly Sunday services and various midweek events. Accept our thanks for the rewarding satisfaction of achievements, whether at small tasks or large. Above all, hear our gratitude for a growing knowledge of you through the spiritual influence of church activities. Grant to each heart the blessing of your enduring peace, that our lives may be a benediction of blessing to others. AMEN.

Christian Prayers
Through the Centuries

For Joy and Gladness

Blessed are Thou, O Lord, who has nourished me from my youth up, who givest food to all flesh. Fill our hearts with joy and gladness that we, always having all sufficiency in all things, may abound to every good work in Christ Jesus our Lord, through whom to Thee be glory, honor, might, majesty and dominion, forever and ever. AMEN.

The Clementine Liturgy
First Century

For Stewardship

O Lord God Almighty, who has built
Thy Church upon the foundation of the
Apostles, under Christ the head corner-
stone, and to this end didst endue Thy
holy apostle St. Barnabas with the singular
gift of the Holy Ghost; leave me not desti-
tute, I humbly beseech Thee, of Thy mani-
fold gifts and talents, nor yet of grace to
make a right use of them always without
any sordid self-ends, to Thy honour and
glory; that, making a due improvement of
all those gifts Thou graciously entrustest
me with, I may be able to give a good
account of my stewardship when the great
Judge shall appear, the Lord Jesus Christ,
who reigneth with Thee and the Eternal
Spirit, one God, blessed forever. AMEN.

Barnabas
Second Century

66

Prayer for God's Help

Give perfection to beginners, O Father; give intelligence to the little ones; give aid to those who are running their course. Give sorrow to the negligent; give fervor of spirit to the lukewarm. Give to the perfect a good consummation; for the sake of Christ Jesus our Lord. AMEN.

Irenaeus
Second Century

Morning Prayer

We give thee hearty thanks for the rest of the past night, and for the gift of a new day, with its opportunities of pleasing thee. Grant that we may so pass its hours in the perfect freedom of thy service, that at eventide we may again give thanks unto thee; through Jesus Christ our Lord. AMEN.

The Eastern Church
Third Century

Christ, Be with Me

Christ, be with me, Christ before me,
    Christ behind me,
Christ in me, Christ beneath me, Christ
    above me,
Christ on my right, Christ on my left.
Christ when I lie, Christ when I sit, Christ
    when I arise,
Christ in the heart of every one who
    thinks of me,
Christ in the mouth of every one who
    speaks of me,
Christ in every eye that sees me.
Christ in every ear that hears me.
    Salvation is of the Lord,
    Salvation is of the Christ,
    May your salvation, O Lord, be ever with
        us.

St. Patrick

Daily Prayer of Thomas Aquinas

Grant me, I beseech Thee, O merciful God, prudently to study, rightly to understand, and perfectly to fulfill that which is pleasing to Thee, to the praise and glory of Thy name.

Thou, O Christ, art the King of glory; Thou art the everlasting Son of the Father. AMEN.

Thomas Aquinas
Thirteenth Century

Praising God of Many Names

O burning Mountain, O chosen Sun,
O perfect Moon, O fathomless Well,
O unattainable Height, O Clearness
    beyond Measure,
O Wisdom without end, O Mercy without
    limit,
O Strength beyond resistance, O Crown
    beyond all majesty:
The humblest thing you created sings your
    praise. AMEN.

Mechtil of Magdelburg
Germany, Thirteenth Century

Prayer for Friends

Almighty, everlasting God, have mercy on Thy servants our friends. Keep them continually under Thy protection, and direct them according to Thy gracious favour in the way of everlasting salvation; that they may desire such things as please Thee, and with all their strength perform the same. And forasmuch as they trust in Thy mercy, vouchsafe, O Lord, graciously to assist them with Thy heavenly help, that they may ever diligently serve Thee, and by no temptations be separated from Thee; through Jesus Christ our Lord. AMEN.

Thomas à Kempis
Fifteenth Century

The Sufficiency of God

God, of your goodness give me yourself;
for you are sufficient for me. I cannot prop-
erly ask anything less, to be worthy of you.
If I were to ask less I should always be in
want. In you alone do I have all. AMEN.

Julian of Norwich
Fifteenth Century

For Overcoming Adversity

Lord, we pray not for tranquility,
    nor that our tribulations may cease;
we pray for thy spirit and thy love,
    that thou grant us strength and
    grace to overcome adversity;
        through Jesus Christ. AMEN.

Girolamo Savonarola
Fifteenth Century

Give Me Grace

Give me thy grace, good Lord,
To set the world at nought,
To set my mind fast on thee.
And not to hang upon the blast of men's
　　mouths.
To be content to be solitary,
Not to long for worldly company,
Little and little utterly to cast off the
　　world,
And rid my mind of all the business
　　thereof.
Gladly to be thinking of God,
Piteously to call for his help,
To lean upon the comfort of God,
Busily to labor to love him.

　　　　　　　　　Thomas More
　　　　　　　　　Sixteenth Century

Teach Me to Be Generous

Dearest Lord, teach me to be generous;
Teach me to serve thee as thou deservest;
To give and not to count the cost,
To fight and not to heed the wounds,
To toil and not to seek for rest,
To labour and not to seek reward,
Save that of knowing that I do thy will.

Ignatius of Loyola
Sixteenth Century

Morning Prayer

We give thanks unto thee, heavenly Father, through Jesus Christ thy dear Son, that thou hast protected us through the night from all danger and harm; and we beseech thee to preserve and keep us, this day also, from all sin and evil; that in all our thoughts, words, and deeds, we may serve and please thee. Into thy hands we commend our bodies and souls, and all that is ours. Let thy holy angel have charge concerning us that the wicked one have no power over us. AMEN.

Martin Luther
Sixteenth Century

For Peace

In these our days so perilous,
Lord, peace in mercy send us;
No God but thee can fight for us,
No God but thee defend us;
  Thou our only God and Savior.

Martin Luther
Sixteenth Century

For Faith

O God, where would we be if thou shouldest forsake us? What can we do if thou withdrawest thy hand? What can we know if thou never enlightenest? How quickly the learned become babes; the prudent, simple; and the wise, fools! How terrible art thou in all thy works and judgments! Let us walk in the light while we have it, so that darkness may not overcome us. Many renounce their faith and become careless and weary of thy grace. Deceived by Satan into thinking they know everything and have no need, they feel satisfied and thus become slothful and ungrateful, and are soon corrupted. Therefore, help us to remain in the ardor of faith that we may daily increase in it through Jesus Christ our real and only Helper. AMEN.

Martin Luther
Sixteenth Century

For Imitation of Christ

Almighty God, inasmuch as thou hast been pleased to set before us an example of every perfection in thine only-begotten Son, grant that we may study to form ourselves in imitation of him. May we follow not only what he has prescribed, but also what he performed, that we may truly prove ourselves to be his members, and thus confirm our adoption. May we so proceed in the whole course of our life that we may at length be gathered into that blessed rest which the same, thine only-begotten Son, hath obtained for us by his own blood. AMEN.

John Calvin
Sixteenth Century

Reliance on God

O Lord,
never suffer us to think
that we can stand by ourselves,
and not need thee.

John Donne
Seventeenth Century

In Thy Service

Thou art never weary, O Lord, of doing us good. Let us never be weary of doing thee service. But, as thou hast pleasure in the prosperity of thy servants, so let us take pleasure in the service of our Lord, and abound in thy work, and in thy love and praise evermore. O fill up all that is wanting, reform whatever is amiss in us, perfect the thing that concerneth us. Let the witness of thy pardoning love ever abide in all our hearts.

John Wesley
Eighteenth Century

For a Lively Spirit

Deliver me, O God, from a slothful mind, from all lukewarmness and all dejection of spirit. I know these cannot but deaden my life to thee; mercifully free my heart from them, and give me a lively, zealous, active and cheerful spirit that I may vigorously perform whatever thou commandest and be ever ardent to obey in all things thy holy love.

John Wesley
Eighteenth Century

Prayer

Only, O Lord, in Thy dear love
Fit us for perfect rest above:
And help us this and every day,
To live more nearly as we pray.

John Keble
Nineteenth Century

For Peace

O Lord, support us all the day long of
this troublous life, until the shadows
lengthen, and the evening comes, and the
busy world is hushed, and the fever of life
is over, and our work is done. Then, in
Thy great mercy, grant us a safe lodging,
and a holy rest, and peace at the last;
through Jesus Christ our Lord. AMEN.

John Henry Newman
Nineteenth Century

To the Holy Spirit

As the wind is thy symbol
so forward our goings.
As the dove
so launch us heavenwards.
As water
so purify our spirits.
As a cloud
so abate our temptations.
As dew
so revive our languor.
As fire
so purge out our dross.

Christina Rossetti
Nineteenth Century

Thy Greatness

God in Heaven, let me really feel my nothingness, not in order to despair over it, but in order to feel the more powerfully the greatness of Thy goodness.

Søren Kierkegaard
Nineteenth Century

Waking

Father in Heaven! When the thought of Thee wakes in our hearts let it not awaken like a frighten bird that flies about in dismay, but like a child waking from its sleep with a heavenly smile.

Søren Kierkegaard
Nineteenth Century

For Illumination

Open wide the window of our spirits, O
Lord, and fill us full of light; open wide the
door of our hearts, that we may receive
and entertain thee with all our powers of
adoration and love. AMEN.

Christina Rossetti
Nineteenth Century

My Heart

Father, into thy hands I give the heart
Which left thee but to learn how good
thou art.

George MacDonald
Twentieth Century

In Praise of the Night

O Lord, we praise Thee for our sister, the Night, who folds all the tired folk of the earth in her comfortable robe of darkness and gives them sleep. Release now the strained limbs of toil and smooth the brow of care. Grant us the refreshing draught of forgetfulness, that we may rise in the morning with a smile on our face. Comfort and ease those who toss wakeful on a bed of pain, or those whose aching nerves crave sleep and find it not. Save them from evil or despondent thoughts in the long darkness, and teach them so to lean on Thy all-pervading life and love, that their souls may grow tranquil and their bodies, too, may rest. And now, through Thee we send Good Night to all our brothers and sisters near and far, and pray for peace upon all the earth. AMEN.

Walter Rauschenbusch
Twentieth Century

For the Spirit of Truth

From the cowardice that dares not face
    new truth,
from the laziness that is contented with
    half-truth,
from the arrogance that thinks it knows all
    truth,
Good Lord, deliver me. AMEN.

Prayer from Kenya

A Refuge Amid Distraction

Like an ant on a stick both ends of which
   are burning,
      I go to and fro without knowing what
to do,
      and in great despair.
Like the inescapable shadow that follows
   me,
      the dead weight of sin haunts me.
Graciously look upon me.
Thy love is my refuge. AMEN.

                              Traditional
                              India

For the Unity of Christ's Body

Help each of us, gracious God,
    to live in such magnanimity and restraint
that the Head of the church may never have
cause to say to any one of us,
    "This is my body, broken by you." AMEN.

Chinese Prayer

For Protection at Night

Dear Jesus, as a hen covers her chicks with her wings to keep them safe, do thou this night protect us under your golden wings. AMEN.

Traditional
India

For a Peaceful Night

O God, you have let me pass the day in
    peace;
let me pass the night in peace, O Lord who
    has no Lord.
There is no strength but in you. You alone
    have no obligation.
Under your hand I pass the night.
You are my Mother and my Father. AMEN.

Traditional prayer of the Boran people